MOUNTAINS

Rebecca Kahn

W
FRANKLIN WATTS
LONDON • SYDNEY

CONTENTS

page 26
page 2
page 18
page 22
page 20

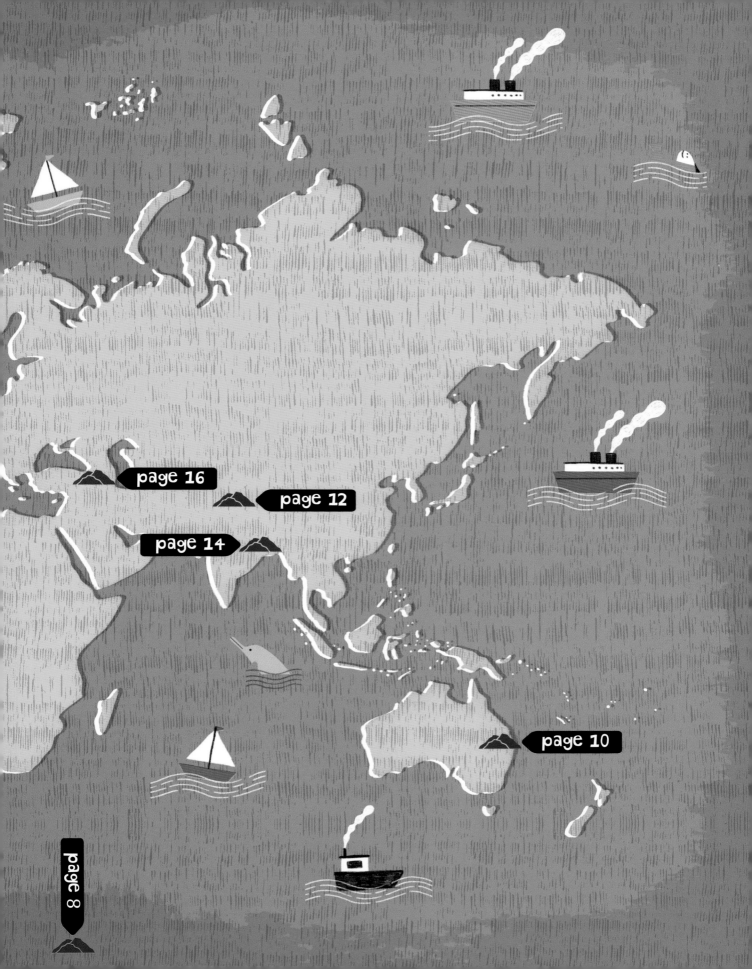

FEATURES OF A MOUNTAIN

A mountain is a landform that rises up much higher than the landscape around it. They are formed of rocks, minerals and soil, and may be covered in ice and snow, deep forests or lush vegetation.

While every mountain range is different, and was formed under different conditions, there are some features that most mountains share. The following terms are important for a better understanding of mountains.

RANGE

A mountain range is a series of mountains that connect together to form a long line of mountains. The longest mountain range in the world is the Andes, which stretches for over 7,000 km.

The Andes Mountains run down the west side of South America, passing through several countries.

RIDGE

A long, narrow raised part of a mountain where the land slopes away steeply on each side.

A narrow path along a mountain ridge in the Carpathian Mountains, Slovakia.

A view of several peaks in the Rocky Mountains, Colorado, USA.

PEAK

A high point on a mountain. A mountain can have several peaks but only one summit (see below).

SUMMIT

The summit is the highest point on a mountain. Depending on how the mountain formed, the summit may have a flat top or a sharp point.

The Matterhorn is a mountain with a pointed summit on the border between Switzerland and Italy.

GLACIERS

A glacier is a slow-moving frozen river of ice. As it moves, it pulls rocks and soil along with it, shaping the landscape beneath the glacier.

This glacier is in Iceland.

VALLEY

The low area, or dip, between two mountains or hills is called a valley. Most valleys were formed thousands or even millions of years ago by the action of rivers or glaciers.

A valley in the Swiss Alps.

SLOPE

A slope is the name for the side of a mountain. Some mountains have gentle slopes while others have steep slopes.

Slopes can be shaped by rivers flowing through them, glaciers sliding down them or from large rock falls.

In winter, these mountain slopes in Romania are fun for skiers.

PLATEAU

A plateau is a large flat area of land, high above sea level. It forms when forces deep within Earth push up the land without causing a fault or a fold (see page 7).

The Tibetan Plateau is a vast area of land in Central and East Asia.

EROSION

Erosion is where forces, such as wind, water and ice, wear away the landscape. For instance, small rocks carried in mountain streams or rivers wear away the mountain surfaces they travel across.

In Jordan, wind and sand have shaped the sandstone mountains.

FOLD MOUNTAINS

A fold mountain forms where two tectonic plates meet each other and cause the Earth's crust to buckle and push upwards. Tectonic plates are the huge slabs of solid rock that make up Earth's crust and float on the mantle.

The Himalayas were created by tectonic plates pushing against each other.

VOLCANIC MOUNTAINS

A volcanic mountain forms when magma (molten rock) escapes through the Earth's crust and piles up on itself.

Mount Kilimanjaro in Tanzania is the highest mountain in Africa and is a dormant volcano.

DOME MOUNTAIN

A dome mountain forms when magma escapes through the Earth's crust. It pushes up, forming a dome-shaped bulge. Over many years, the magma cools, forming hard rock.

Bear Butte in South Dakota, USA is a dome mountain.

FAULT-BLOCK MOUNTAINS

Fault-block mountains form over millions of years as a result of tectonic plates moving towards each other. The force of the plates' movement causes cracks, known as fault lines, to develop along lines of weakness in the Earth's crust. Along the fault lines, huge blocks of rock are forced upwards, or sometimes downwards.

Yosemite National Park, California, USA has good examples of fault-block mountains.

THE TRANSANTARCTIC MOUNTAINS

The Transantarctic Mountains (or TAM for short) stretch for over 3,000 km from one end of the Antarctic continent to the other and mark the boundary between East and West Antarctica. Many explorers have had to cross the mountains in order to reach the South Pole.

DINOSAURS

The highest peak in the TAM is Mount Kirkpatrick, which is 4,558 m above sea level. It is generally free from ice and snow, which makes it ideal for fossil hunting. Several important fossils of plant-eating dinosaurs have been found on the peak, which prove that Antarctica was once covered in forests.

ANCIENT PEAKS

The TAM are much older than other mountains in Antarctica. By studying the layers of sediment and rocks that make up the TAM, geologists estimate that they were formed during the Cenozoic period, about 65 million years ago.

FIRST SIGHT

The TAM were first recorded by the British explorer James Clark Ross in 1841. From 1901-1904 Captain Robert Falcon Scott and his party were the first to cross them during the Discovery Expedition. In the 1950s, explorers used aerial photos to map the range, and it was officially named in 1960.

EXPLORED BY AIR

The TAM are an important part of the scientific research that takes place in Antarctica. Each year, NASA's Operation IceBridge uses scientific instruments in planes to record glaciers, ice sheets and sea ice in the Antarctic and Arctic in order to learn more about climate change.

FROZEN DESERT

The McMurdo Dry Valleys are in the southern end of the range. These have no snow or ice in them. The mountains prevent ice from glaciers entering the valleys, and the area has very low rainfall. This makes them one of the few places in Antarctica not covered in ice, and also one of the driest places on Earth.

LITTLE LIFE

The summits and valleys of the TAM are so cold and dry that very few species live there. Lichens and fungi are all that can survive in the harsh climate. This makes the mountains a good substitute for scientists who are studying ways in which life might be supported on Mars.

a close-up of lichen

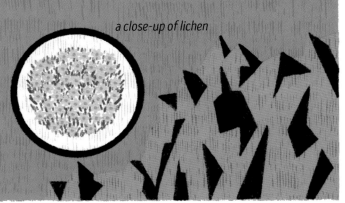

THE GREAT DIVIDING RANGE

The Great Dividing Range is the longest mountain range in Australia. It runs down the east coast from Duan Island, off the coast of Queensland, to Victoria. It's not one range of mountains but a collection of mountain ranges, plateaus and escarpments, marked by deep gorges.

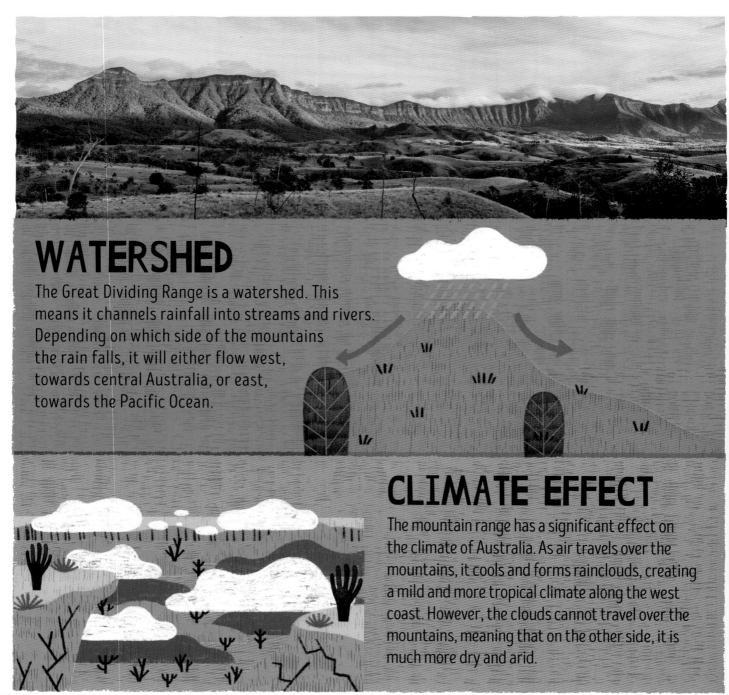

WATERSHED

The Great Dividing Range is a watershed. This means it channels rainfall into streams and rivers. Depending on which side of the mountains the rain falls, it will either flow west, towards central Australia, or east, towards the Pacific Ocean.

CLIMATE EFFECT

The mountain range has a significant effect on the climate of Australia. As air travels over the mountains, it cools and forms rainclouds, creating a mild and more tropical climate along the west coast. However, the clouds cannot travel over the mountains, meaning that on the other side, it is much more dry and arid.

RARE ANIMALS

The mountains are home to several species of animal that are not found anywhere else, because their mountain habitats are so isolated and difficult to cross. Tiger quolls and long-nosed potoroos are marsupials that live in the eastern highlands of the mountains.

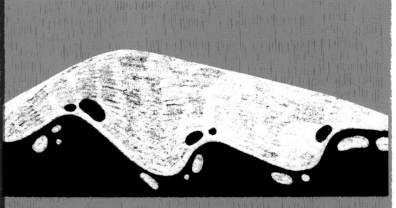

long-nosed potoroo

tiger quoll

OLD AS THE HILLS

The highest peak in the Great Dividing Range is Mount Kosciuszko, which stands 2,228 m above sea level. Aboriginal Australians call the mountain Jar-gan-gil, which means Table Top Mountain. It is one of the few places in Australia where it regularly snows.

TUNNELS

In the 19th century, European settlers and their descendants wanted to improve transport connections to the west of the Great Dividing Range. They built railways across the mountains at several points. This meant building some tunnels, including Muntapa Tunnel in Queensland.

ANCIENT INHABITANTS

Aboriginal Australians have been living in the southern part of the range, which runs through New South Wales, for over 20,000 years. Ancient Aboriginal rock art, such as hand prints, can be found near the village of Ulan.

THE KUNLUN MOUNTAINS

The Kunlun Mountains form one of the longest mountain ranges in Asia, running for 3,000 km from Siberia into China and Mongolia. They are a unique combination of volcanic and fault-block mountains.

HIGH POINT

The highest point in the Kunlun Mountains is Kongur Tagh, which is 7,649 m above sea level. The first documented ascent of Kongur Tagh was made by a group of British climbers in 1981.

HIGH, HOT AND COLD

While the highest peaks are covered in glaciers and snow, the Kunlun Mountains are known as a dry range, as they do not get much rain or snow, and there are few rivers. On the south side, the high altitude, strong winds and lack of rainfall mean the region is almost uninhabited. On the northern side of the range, the Gobi Desert has extremely hot summers and very cold winters.

yak

ibex

wild ass

brown bear

ANIMAL LIFE

The harsh climate means that plants struggle to grow on the mountains, yet some grazing animals, including wild yaks and asses, manage to find enough to eat. More wildlife is found on the western side of the mountains, including ibex and brown bears.

FEW CROSSINGS

The Kunlun are mountains remote and inaccessible. Only two roads and one railway line cross the range along its 3,000 km length, and all other crossings have to be attempted by foot.

KUNLUN SHAN

Kunlun Shan is a mythical mountain range in Chinese mythology based on the Kunlun Mountains. Kunlan Shan is the earthly home of gods, goddesses and sacred animals.

PRECIOUS STONES

Jade from the Kunlun Mountains is prized in China because of its delicate green and white patterns. During the 2008 Beijing Olympics, all the medals awarded to the winners featured a disc of Kunlun jade on the back.

THE HIMALAYAS

The Himalayas are a range of mountains that separate the Indian subcontinent from the Tibetan Plateau. The range runs for 2,400 km from Pakistan in the west to China in the east. It has the highest mountain in the world, Mount Everest, at 8,848 m.

YOUNG MOUNTAINS

The Himalayas are only 50 million years old, making them some of the youngest mountains on Earth. They are fold mountains, formed when two tectonic plates collided. As these plates are still moving, the mountains continue to grow by about 1 cm a year, causing earthquakes from time to time.

SEA STONES

The summit of Mount Everest was once on the sea floor! Geologists know this as it is formed of marine limestone.

FROZEN WATER

After the Arctic and the Antarctic, the Himalayas have the third largest amount of ice and snow, mostly stored in its 15,000 glaciers. Meltwater from some of these glaciers feeds some of the world's greatest rivers, including the Ganges and the Yangtze.

ENDANGERED SPECIES

The Himalayas have a varied climate, ranging from tropical in the foothills to permanent ice and snow on the peaks. This diversity makes them home to many rare and endangered species, including red pandas, Himalayan brown bears, golden langur monkeys and snow leopards.

golden langur

Himalayan brown bear

red panda

snow leopard

MOUNTAIN NATIONS

The Himalayas stretch across northern India, Pakistan, Afghanistan and China, as well as Nepal and Bhutan. For thousands of years, the mountains provided natural barriers to protect Nepal and Bhutan from outsiders. In the 17th century, the kings of Bhutan built huge fortresses on mountain peaks to add to their country's defences.

SACRED PLACES

People of many faiths make pilgrimages to the Himalayas. They worship at sacred sites, including temples, shrines and monasteries, on the steep mountain slopes.

THE CAUCASUS

The Caucasus are a range of mountains in Asia that run between the Black Sea and the Caspian Sea, and cross Russia, Georgia, Armenia and Azerbaijan. Throughout history, the Caucasus have been seen as the dividing line between Europe to the west of the mountains and Asia to the east.

FORMATION

The Greater Caucasus in the north are fold mountains, formed when two tectonic plates collided million of years ago. The Lesser Caucasus in the south are mostly volcanic mountains. This area still regularly experiences earthquakes due to volcanic activity.

HIGHEST PEAK

Mount Elbrus, the highest mountain in Europe, is part of the Caucasus range. The mountain is a dormant volcano in southern Russia. Geologists think it last erupted in about CE 50.

ROMAN EMPIRE

Under Emperor Pompey, the Roman army conquered all the land up to the northern slopes of the Lesser Caucasus in 65 BCE. A Roman bridge, named 'Pompey's Bridge', still spans the Aragvi river in Georgia, on the southern slopes of the mountains.

SILK ROAD

The Caucasus were an important part of the Silk Road, a network of trade routes between the Mediterranean and China, which first emerged in about 120 BCE. Goods carried on camels, donkeys and horses were traded along the route, which ran along the edge of deserts and through river valleys.

GREEN MOUNTAINS

The climate of the Caucasus varies from subtropical marshlands at lower levels to glaciers higher up. While most of the higher peaks are covered in ice and snow, the lower slopes have forests of pine, oak, ash and birch trees.

UNDERGROUND RICHES

The rock layers around the Greater Caucasus contain rich oil, natural gas and coal deposits. Iron, copper and manganese are also mined along the accessible parts of the range in Georgia and Russia.

THE ATLAS MOUNTAINS

The Atlas Mountains are in North Africa. They run east to west across the continent, through Morocco, Algeria and Tunisia. They separate the Mediterranean and Atlantic coastlines in the north from the Sahara Desert to the south. The highest peak in the Atlas is Toubkal, in Morocco.

OLD AND FOLDED

The Atlas Mountains are fold mountains (see page 7). Some parts of the Atlas, such as the Tell Atlas, are still growing and experience frequent earthquakes.

FROM SNOW TO SAND

The Atlas are divided into four regions: the High Atlas in Morocco; the Tell Atlas that cross Morocco, Algeria and Tunisia; the eastern Aurè in Algeria and Tunisia; and the Saharan Atlas at the northern edge of the desert. The High Atlas receive regular snowfall, which makes them a popular skiing destination, while the Sahara Atlas are dry and surrounded by sandy desert.

ORIGINAL INHABITANTS

The Berber people have lived in the Atlas Mountains for at least 4,000 years. They have preserved their ancient culture and language, despite many attempts by invaders to take over their lands. Today, most Berbers live in villages in the mountains.

RAIN BARRIER

The high peaks of the Atlas act as a weather barrier between the Mediterranean's mild climate north of the range, and the harsh heat and cold nights of the Sahara Desert to the south. This gives the northern side of the mountains milder weather, allowing plants to grow, but also blocks rain clouds from moving further south.

PRECIOUS ROCKS

The Atlas Mountains have lots of natural resources and precious metals, such as silver, iron ore, copper, mercury, phosphate and marble. The Berber people are famous for their jewellery made with local silver.

Cuvier's gazelle

Barbary leopard

Barbary macaque

RARE SPECIES

Most of the Atlas Mountains have few plants so not many animals can live there. Those that do are extremely rare and endangered. They include Barbary macaque monkeys, Barbary leopards and Cuvier's gazelles.

THE ANDES

The Andes are the longest mountain range in the world. They run north to south along the west side of South America, crossing seven countries: Venezuela, Colombia, Ecuador, Peru, Bolivia, Argentina and Chile. The highest peak is Aconcagua at 6,959 m.

VOLCANOS

The Andes are fold mountains, formed by the meeting of the Nazca and South American tectonic plates between 250 and 66 million years ago. The range still has some active volcanoes, hot springs and geysers, particularly in Chile.

CLIMATE

The climate of the Andes varies a great deal. The Tropical Andes, which run through Venezuela, Colombia, Ecuador, Peru and Bolivia, are covered in rainforests and cloud forests. The Dry Andes in Chile and Argentina include some of the driest places on Earth, such as the Atacama Desert in Chile.

MACHU PICCHU

In the 15th century, the Inca Empire flourished in the Central Andes. The Inca built the citadel of Machu Picchu on a ridge of the Andes near the city of Cuzco in Peru, over 2,400 m above sea level.

PACK ANIMALS

Parts of the Andes are too remote for cars and other vehicles to access. The people who live there still use llamas and alpacas for transporting goods through the mountain passes. Alpaca wool is also used for knitting and weaving warm clothes.

alpaca

llama

MOUNTAIN FARMS

People living in the Andes carved terraces out of the mountain slopes to grow crops such as maize, beans, potatoes, cotton and coffee.

SILVER MOUNTAINS

The Andes became famous around the world when the Spanish conquistadors arrived in South America in the 16th century and began mining the mountains for gold, silver and copper to transport back to Europe. Some of the world's richest silver mines are still found in the Andes.

THE ROCKIES

The Rocky Mountains, often called the Rockies, are a mountain range that stretches from British Colombia in western Canada to New Mexico in Southwest USA. The highest summit in the Rockies is Mount Elbert, in Colorado, USA, at 4,401 m.

MIXED ROCKS

The Rockies were formed between 80 and 55 million years ago, when plate tectonics created these fold mountains. Because they are fold mountains, the Rockies contain many different types of rock, including sedimentary, volcanic and igneous rocks.

GRASS AND ROCKS

The landscape varies a great deal, from meadows, prairies and grasslands at lower levels to pine forests and rocky, snow-bound tundra high on the slopes.

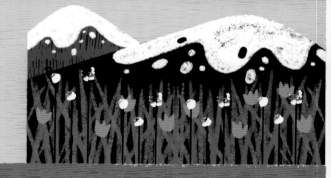

FIRST NATIONS

Many indigenous people lived in and along the Rockies. Cheyenne, Blackfoot, Crow Nation and Sioux tribes hunted bison, mountain goats and big horn sheep on the slopes. Rock walls that they built to drive herds back still stand in some places.

MOUNTAIN PASS

Thousands of settlers passed through the Rockies using the Oregon Trail, which was a path taken by people travelling from the centre of the USA to the west coast during the 19th century. The South Pass, used by Native American Indians for thousands of years, allowed settlers to drive their wagons across the mountains in Wyoming.

MOUNTAIN PARKS

The Rockies contain 13 National Parks - eight in the USA and five in Canada. The most famous is Yellowstone National Park in the USA. It sits on top of a supervolcano and has lots of hot springs and geysers including Old Faithful, a geyser that erupts every 35 to 120 minutes, shooting hot water 32-56 m into the air.

MINING THE MOUNTAINS

The Rockies contain large deposits of copper, gold, lead, gas, oil and silver. Some of the largest coal mines in Canada are situated on the slopes of the Rockies and there are many mines on the USA side of the mountain range.

THE ALPS

The Alps are a mountain range in Central Europe that stretches across eight different countries: Slovenia, Germany, Austria, Liechtenstein, Monaco, Italy, Switzerland and France. The range is 1,200 km long, and the highest peak is Mont Blanc.

CLIMATE

The Alps have a significant effect on the weather of the European countries around them. The snow and glaciers on the high peaks keep the regions around the mountains cooler. Meltwater flows into streams, rivers and lakes. The snow and glaciers are also popular places for skiers and snowboarders.

PLATES COLLIDE

The Alps are fold mountains, formed over millions of years as the African and Eurasian tectonic plates slowly collided. Sedimentary rocks were forced upwards and folded to form high mountain peaks.

ELEPHANTS OVER THE ALPS

During the Second Punic War (218-201 BCE) between the Roman Empire and the Carthaginians, Hannibal, the leader of the Carthaginians, led thousands of men, horses and elephants across the Alps to attack the Romans in Italy. Historians continue to research his exact route.

VINEYARDS

On the sunny, south-facing slopes of the Alps, farmers grow grapes to make wine. Higher up, they graze cows, goats and sheep in the warmer months and grow crops in the valley floors.

ROADS OVER THE ALPS

The Alps are crossed by many roads and railway lines, which travel through the valleys and over the slopes. However, some villages are very isolated and can only be reached by cable car or small, specially built cog railway lines.

SNOWSULATION

In some parts of the Alps, people build their houses (called chalets) with roofs made from Alpine rocks. The roofs have to be built at a particular angle, in order to keep a layer of snow on them during the winter. This acts as extra insulation from the cold.

THE GRAMPIANS

The Grampian Mountains are a mountain range in the Scottish Highlands. They run diagonally across Scotland and form part of the boundary with England. The highest peak in the United Kingdom, Ben Nevis, and the second highest peak, Ben Macdui, are both part of the Grampian range.

GREY GRANITE

The mountain range formed about 480–440 million years ago when the movement of tectonic plates caused a chain of volcanic islands to collide with the Grampian Highlands. Molten rock formed and escaped through the Earth's crust to form mountains of hard-wearing granite. The granite is famous for smoky grey quartz crystals.

BAG A MOUNTAIN

In Scotland, mountains that are over 914.4 m high are called Munros. They are named after Sir Hugh Munro, the first person to make a list of these mountains in 1891. There are 282 in total, with 18 in the Grampian Mountains. Mountaineers say they have 'bagged a Munro' when they climb one.

LAKES AND RIVERS

During the Ice Age, the Grampian Mountains were shaped by the movement of glaciers, which carved deep valleys out of the rock. When they melted, the water created deep lakes, such as Loch Ness.

COLD MOUNTAINS

The Grampians are some of the coldest places in the UK, and this makes them a tough place to live. The weather conditions on Ben Nevis can change suddenly from sunny and warm to foggy and cold, bringing danger to climbers.

RARE WILDLIFE

Wide open spaces, moors and forests provide homes for plenty of animals and plants. Animals that are rare elsewhere in the UK thrive here, including red squirrels, otters and Scottish wildcats.

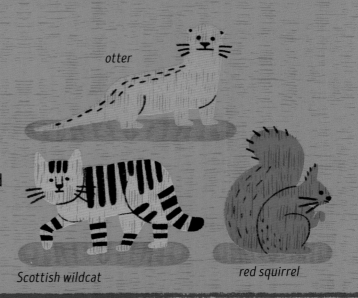

otter

Scottish wildcat

red squirrel

ANCIENT BATTLE

In CE 84 the ancient Romans fought the Battle of Mons Graupius in the Grampian Mountains and defeated the Caledonian tribes of what is now Scotland. After that, most of the tribes accepted Roman rule but others continued to rebel. The Romans built two defensive walls - Hadrian's Wall and the Antonine Wall to protect themselves.

STUDYING MOUNTAINS

MONTOLOGY

It takes many different experts to study a mountain. The study of mountains is known as montology, or orology. Geologists investigate the rocks and minerals that make up mountains, while volcanologists study volcanoes. Botanists are interested in the plant life of a mountain, while biologists look at all the living things on a mountain.

Geologists study mountain rocks to investigate how they formed.

CLIMATE CHANGE

Montologists who study glaciers are called glaciologists. They study how glaciers affect the planet and monitor any changes. This is particularly important in relation to climate change as glaciers are very sensitive to small rises in air temperature.

This glaciologist is setting up monitoring equipment on a glacier in Greenland.

ALTITUDE ADAPTATIONS

All living things need oxygen to survive. However, on top of high mountains, there is less oxygen, which can affect the human body. At high-altitude research stations on mountains around the world, doctors study how people have adapted to living high in mountain communities.

Researchers have discovered that Nepalese Sherpas have adapted to living at high altitudes. These Sherpas are carrying climbers' equipment up a mountain.

Volcanologists at work in the crater of Mount Teide on Tenerife, part of the Canary Islands.

MONITORING MOUNTAINS

Mountains may appear solid and still but they are continually being shaped by the forces of nature. Deep in the Earth, plate tectonics can push them upwards, while wind, rain and rivers are constantly eroding them. These powerful forces sometimes cause dramatic natural disasters, such as earthquakes, landslides and avalanches.

BLAST OFF!

From August 2015 until August 2016, six scientists lived in a small dome-shaped tent on the slopes of a volcanic mountain in Hawaii, in order to simulate the conditions of living on Mars. The altitude of the mountain, and the rocky, dry conditions were some of the closest they could find to what life on Mars might be like.

GLOSSARY

Aborigine One of the native people of Australia who lived there before European settlers arrived from the late 18th century onwards.

adapted How an inherited feature allows a plant or animal to survive in its environment.

altitude The height of something above sea level.

climate The usual weather for a place.

climate change The large-scale change in Earth's weather patterns and average air temperatures.

conquistador One of the 16th century Spanish soldier invaders of Mexico and Peru.

continent One of Earth's seven main divisions of land. They are Asia, Africa, North America, South America, Antarctica, Europe and Australia.

crust In this book, Earth's crust, the outer layer of the Earth's surface.

dome mountain A mountain formed of hardened magma that has pushed its way up under Earth's crust.

earthquake A sudden shaking of the ground caused by movements within Earth's crust.

endangered animal An animal that is in danger of dying out and becoming extinct.

erosion The process that wears rocks down through the action of wind, rain and ice.

escarpment A long, steep slope, especially at the edge of a plateau.

fault A crack in Earth's crust.

fault-block mountain A mountain formed when two tectonic plates move towards each other, causing Earth's crust to crack along fault lines. Within the fault lines, huge blocks of rock are forced upwards.

First Nations Any of the original (indigenous) peoples of Canada who lived there before settlers arrived from Europe.

fold mountain A mountain formed when two tectonic plates move towards each other, pushing Earth's crust up.

foothill A low hill at the bottom of a mountain.

geyser A hot spring that regularly boils, sending a tall column of hot water and steam into the air.

glacier A slow-moving river of ice.

gorge A deep valley with steep rocky sides.

habitat The place and living conditions that a plant or animal prefers to live in.

igneous rock A type of rock that forms when molten material (magma) from within the Earth cools to form crystals.

inaccessible Difficult to reach.

magma Molten rock in the Earth's core.

mantle The thick layer of semi-molten rock that sits around Earth's core, and under Earth's crust.

marine limestone This is a type of sedimentary rock that formed on the sea floor and is mostly made up of the dead remains of small sea animals and plants.

molten In liquid form.

National Park An area of land that is protected by a national government due to its natural beauty, or because it has a special history.

peak A high point on a mountain.

plate One of the huge sections of land and rock that form the Earth's crust.

plate tectonics The movement of the tectonic plates, which float on Earth's mantle.

plateau A plateau is a large flat area of land, high above sea level

prairie A large open area of grassland, especially in Canada and the northern states of the USA.

sedimentary rock A type of rock formed from the broken remains of other rocks that, over millions of years, settle on a seabed (or the bottom of a lake), and build up in layers.

Sherpa One of a group of people who have lived high in the mountains of Nepal for thousands of years.
summit The highest point on a mountain.

Taoist A follower of Taoism, an ancient Chinese religion.
tundra A large area of land without trees, found in cold, northern areas.

FURTHER INFORMATION

Books

At Home in the Biome: Mountains by Louise and Richard Spilsbury (Wayland)
Expedition Diaries: Himalayan Mountains by Simon Chapman (Franklin Watts)
Fact Planet:Mountains by Izzi Howell (Franklin Watts)
Geographics: Mountains by Izzi Howell (Franklin Watts)

Websites

The Royal Geographical Society's teaching resources about mountains, volcanoes and earthquakes:
www.rgs.org/schools/teaching-resources/mountains,-volcanoes-and-earthquakes
Discover more about the geology of Britain with the British Geological Survey:
www.bgs.ac.uk/discoveringGeology/geologyOfBritain/home.html
This Australian Government website has classroom resources about Australia's geoscience:
www.ga.gov.au/education/classroom-resources
Watch clips from the BBC series Planet Earth Mountains:
www.bbc.co.uk/programmes/b0074sg0/clips
The website of the Mountain Professor:
www.mountainprofessor.com
Learn more about earthquakes at this USGS website:
earthquake.usgs.gov/learn/kids

INDEX

Franklin Watts
First published in Great Britain in 2020
by The Watts Publishing Group
Copyright © The Watts Publishing Group, 2020
All rights reserved

HB ISBN: 978 1 4451 6195 2
PB ISBN: 978 1 4451 6196 9

Editor: Paul Rockett
Illustrator: Paloma Valdivia
Designer: Lisa Peacock
Picture Researcher: Diana Morris

Franklin Watts
An imprint of Hachette Children's Group
Part of The Watts Publishing Group
Carmelite House
50 Victoria Embankment
London EC4Y 0DZ
An Hachette UK Company

The publisher would like to thank the following for permission to reproduce their pictures:

alionabirukova/Shutterstock: 5c; Ammit/Dreamstime: 6t; Aurora Photos/Alamy: 5bl; Citizen of the Planet/Alamy: 29b; Clearviewstock/Shutterstock: 28t; Dominique de la Croix/Shutterstock: 7b; Cassandra Cury/Shutterstock: 10t; Sergey Dzyuba /Shutterstock: 18t; Gioia Forster/DPA/Alamy: 28b; David Hancock/Dreamstime: 20t; Jodi Jacobson/iStockphoto: 4bl; Jonathansphotos/Dreamstime: 14t; Frédéric Maillard/Dreamstime: 6b; nexusimage/iStockphoto: 8t; outcast85/Shutterstock: 6cl; Casaba Peterdi/Shutterstock: 26t; Planet Observer/UIG/Alamy: 7t; Robin Runck/Shutterstock: 7c; Goran Šarafek/Alamy: 6cr; Martinho Smart/Shutterstock: 5tl; Andrzej Stajer/iStockphoto: 4cr; Nguyen Quoc Thang/Shutterstock: 29t; Balthasar Thomass/Alamy: 12t; Vivek BR/Shutterstock: 22t; David Wall/Alamy: 16t; ZGPhotography/Shutterstock: 24t.

Every attempt has been made to clear copyright. Should there be any inadvertent omission please apply to the publisher for rectification.

www.hachette.co.uk
www.hachettechildrens.co.uk

Printed in Dubai